Canals

KATE PETTY and TERRY CASH

Photographs by Ed Barber

Contents

TRACKS

A&C Black · London

Travel by water

Is there a canal near you? Some canals are very busy, with lots of water traffic, while some are peaceful. Others have become choked up with weeds, or even put into pipes, so you might not know they are there.

If you live in a city, there is probably a canal near you. The canals are a network of man-made rivers. A map of the canals looks very like a road map. Canals were links between towns and between rivers.

Two hundred years ago, canals were mainly used for transporting cargo such as coal and building materials between mines and factories.

Today, most people who travel on canals in Britain are on pleasure trips and holidays. But until less than fifty years ago, whole families lived on narrowboats, working many hours a day to carry goods and make a living.

Pulling power

The ancient Egyptians, Chinese and Romans all built canals. The first modern British canal was built in 1761 for transporting coal. At the time, many new factories were being built. The new factory machines were powered by coal, so a quick, cheap way was needed to deliver it.

Soon canals were being built all over the country, to transport food, building materials and many of the things which are now carried by road. Roads in the eighteenth century were muddy tracks, and horse-drawn carriages gave a much bumpier ride than boats. Rivers were useful highways, but canals could transport boats where there wasn't a river, or if the river was difficult to navigate.

On a river barges were powered by wind in their sails, but sailing is usually impossible on a narrow inland canal so narrowboats needed some other form of power.

Nearly all barges were towed by horses, or donkeys or mules, which would walk along the towpath by the side of the canal. Near a lock a man might pull the boat along. A horse can pull a far heavier load on a barge than on a cart. Why do you think this is?

You will need
a bowl of water   a toy boat   some other different surfaces, such as wood.
plasticine   carpet

Pull your boat along several different surfaces. Which one is the easiest? Try the same experiment with some plasticine in the boat as cargo.

Until quite recently horses worked on canals. In the early part of this century, steam boats were used. Nowadays most boats have diesel engines. Some boats, called butties, don't have engines and are pulled by ones that do. Sometimes a tug will pull several boats, and on wider working canals, modern barges can be pushed by a 'push tug'.

Building the canals

When the canals were built, digging machines hadn't been invented. Teams of men used shovels and wheelbarrows to dig out a long trench. A long run of planks was set up so the wheelbarrows didn't sink into the mud. Then the dug-out earth was taken away by cart. The men were called Navvies, because they worked on 'navigations' (the old word for a canal), and the name stuck, even when they went to work on the railways.

The trench for the canal didn't have to be very deep. It was lined with thick clay, called puddle, which made it watertight.

The water for a canal is usually taken from a lake or reservoir at its highest point. The water in a river always flows downwards, and once the canal is filled, it has to be kept level. Otherwise the water would drain away downhill.

However steep or sloping the sides of a canal may be, the water always finds its own level. You can try experimenting with different sorts of bottles, filled with water. What happens if you tilt them?

Look at these drawings. Which water level is wrong?

Aqueducts and tunnels

How did the canal engineers manage to keep the canal level through hilly country? The earliest canals took the long way round and curved round the foot of the hill. But the builders of later canals had more adventurous ideas.

A special kind of bridge, called an aqueduct, can carry a canal across a valley. It's very important that an aqueduct is watertight!

Tunnels were dug to carry a canal under a hill. Shafts were bored into the ground along the route of the tunnel, then men were lowered down them to start digging. It was dangerous work and many navvies were killed: buried alive or hit by rock falls when explosions went wrong.

Canal tunnels are low and narrow, and some are more than 2 km long. In many tunnels there is no towpath. The horse would be led over the top, often by the children, while the boatmen would 'leg' the tunnel themselves or pay 'leggers' to help them. A pair of planks would be laid on the front of the boat, and a man would lie on his back on each plank. The men would then walk along tunnel walls to move the boat along. It could take three hours to 'leg' it through one tunnel.

Locks

You can't travel far on a canal without coming to a lock. A lock is like a stair in the canal – it was a very clever solution to the problem of getting boats up and down hills.

A lock looks like a corridor with doors at each end. This is how a lock works when a boat is travelling downhill:

The top gate is opened and the boat goes in to the lock.

Then both gates are closed. Flaps, called paddles, in the bottom gate are opened and water rushes out.

The water level in the lock goes down, and so does the boat.

When the water level in the lock is the same as in the canal on the other side, the paddles are shut.

The bottom gate is opened and the boat can leave the lock, shutting the gate behind.

A boat travelling uphill goes through the same process in reverse.

Most paddles are opened by a sort of large spanner called a windlass.

Barges and narrowboats

A barge is a flat-bottomed boat built for carrying cargo on rivers and canals. Barges come in different shapes and sizes – at one time different parts of the country had their own types of barge.

A narrowboat is also flat-bottomed for carrying cargo, but is smaller – usually less than 7ft (about 2m) wide. Many British canals are very narrow, with locks only seven feet wide, because the canal builders were anxious to save water.

Unfortunately, this made it very difficult to modernise canals, while roads and railways were widened to take more traffic. When engines were fitted to narrowboats, they took up valuable cargo space, but it wasn't possible to make bigger boats as they wouldn't fit into the locks. Barges began to be used less and less as transport.

There are a few broad canals and waterways in the north and south-west of England which can take large barges with bigger loads. In other parts of the world where the canals and locks are wider, huge amounts of cargo are shifted by barge all the time.

Cargoes

For years before lorries and trains were used, barges and narrowboats carried all sorts of cargo. Sand, gravel, clay, coal, timber and grain could all be loaded straight into the barge. Liquids were transported in barrels. Smooth water transport was also popular with the owners of pottery factories. Why do you think they preferred to use canals rather than bumpy roads?

Modern barges on commercial waterways are still used to carry lots of different cargoes: raw materials from the docks to the factory, and goods from the warehouse to the port. One firm transports barrels of lime juice and another, bicycles.

Cargo has to be loaded carefully:

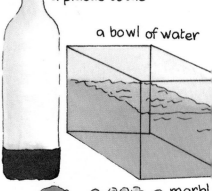

You will need
a plastic bottle
a bowl of water
marbl
plasticine

1. Cut a square shape out of the lemonade bottle. Float the bottle on the water. How stable is it?

2. Now carefully put some plasticine cargo along the bottom of the bottle boat. Does this make it more stable?

3. What happens if you put all the cargo up one end?

4. Or if you put in too much?

Life on the narrowboats

Until forty years ago, whole families lived and worked on the narrowboats. It is hard to imagine how families with several children managed to live in such a tiny space, especially when the weather was bad. The children had to work hard and hardly ever went to school. Life was tough for their mothers who were expected to shop, cook and look after the family as well as help with the boat.

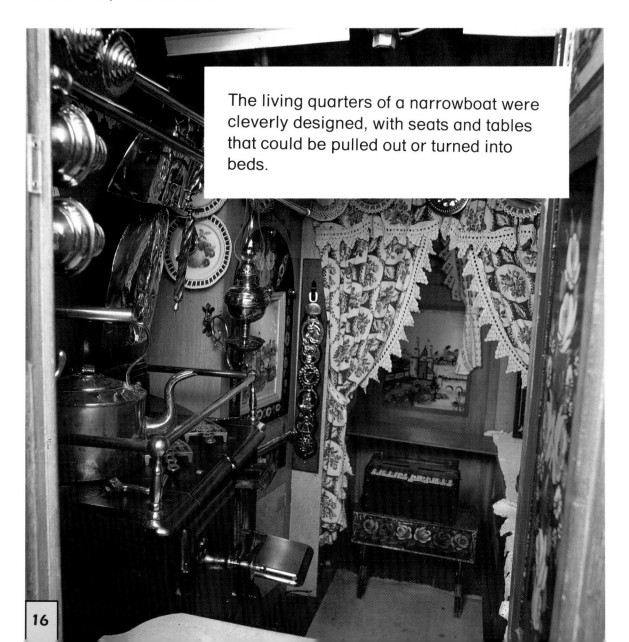

The living quarters of a narrowboat were cleverly designed, with seats and tables that could be pulled out or turned into beds.

Barge people were very proud of their boats and kept them spotless. Traditional narrowboats were beautifully decorated with brightly painted roses and castles, polished brasses and ornamental lace. Elaborate ropework protected the outside from bumps and scrapes. The horse was decorated for special occasions, too. When a well-loved horse died, its tail was fixed to the rudder post for good luck.

This picture shows the inside of a modern narrowboat.

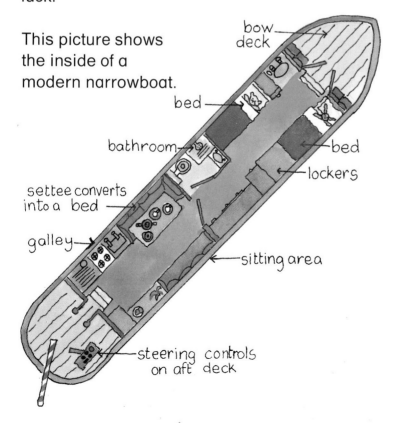

bow deck

bed

bathroom

bed

lockers

settee converts into a bed

galley

sitting area

steering controls on aft deck

Most narrowboats were run by big companies. The few boat owners who worked for themselves were known as 'Number Ones'. Canal families usually didn't mix with other families.

Try designing a living space for yourself which is just 2m × 3m and includes somewhere to eat, sleep, cook, keep your clothes, wash, and go to the toilet.

■ ■ ■ ■ ■ ■ ■ ■ ■ ■
Canal traffic

The big commercial canals, such as the Manchester Ship
Canal, aren't suitable for pleasure boats. But the narrow
canals are used for all kinds of water activities. Because there
is so little working traffic, there is room for windsurfers,
canoeists, and motor boats.

In contrast, the canals of Europe, the USSR and the USA are tremendously busy highways with a constant flow of heavily laden ships and barges.

Some of the big city canals use lifts instead of locks. A boat goes into a special tub full of water which carries it from one level to another. This lift only takes a few minutes – much quicker than going through a lock.

Two canal cities

The main streets of Amsterdam, the capital city of Holland, all run alongside canals. The canals were dug so that ships could deliver goods right up to the door. Wooden posts for cargo hoists still stick out from high up the canalside buildings.

The main streets of Venice, in Italy, *are* canals. Everybody, including the postman, the undertaker and the laundry service, travels by boat. Venice is built on 118 little islands in a lagoon and the city is criss-crossed by 177 canals. Special water buses and taxis called gondolas are used to carry people around.

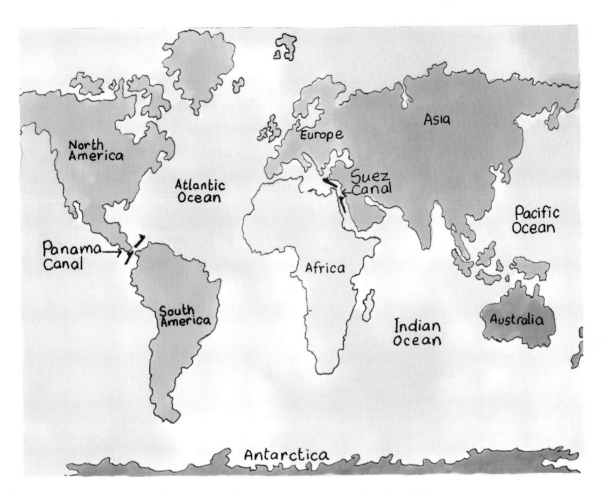

Look at this map of the world. Can you see why the Panama Canal and the Suez Canal are so important to ships? How much longer would their journeys be if they couldn't cut through these canals from one ocean to another?

Both of these canals took over ten years and thousands of men to dig. They had to be deep enough to take huge ships. Each canal has enormous locks at either end.

Because the Suez Canal is so important, it has been fought over several times since it was built. It was closed by the Egyptians for many years and re-opened in 1975.

Canals and conservation

When many canals stopped being used commercially, they became silted up and overgrown with weed. The water became stagnant and murky. Disused city canals, polluted by rubbish and factory waste, become very dangerous places.

Now volunteers are working to open up some of the disused sections again, clearing scrub, rebuilding walls and locks and improving the towpath.

Walkers as well as boaters can enjoy the canals. There is plenty of wildlife to see, even in inner cities. Look out for foxes, kingfishers, moorhens, kestrels and herons, as well as different kinds of ducks and geese.

Some people even hope to find their supper in the canal.

23

■ ■ ■ ■ ■
Facts

The remains of possibly the **oldest** canals are about **6,000 years old**. They were discovered near Mandali in Iraq.

The **longest ancient** canal, the Grand Canal of China, is **1,781 km** long. At one time there were 5,000,000 people building it.

The **longest inland** canal today is **2,300 km**. It is the Volga-Baltic in the USSR.

The Suez Canal is the **longest ship** canal at **161.9 km**.

The **busiest ship canal** is the Kiel Canal, linking the Baltic Sea in Germany with the North Sea, with over **45,000 transits** a year.

The **longest and largest canal tunnel** in the world, now closed, is the Rove Tunnel in the South of France. It is **7,120 m long**, **22 m wide** and **11.4 m high**.

The **longest flight of locks** is at Tardebigge on the Worcester and Birmingham canal. **Thirty-six locks** drop the canal 78.9 m in 4 km.

The **highest boat lift** carries boats up **68.6 m** at Ronquieres in Belgium.

Lock gates
The lock gates on the Panama Canal are each 25 m high, 2.1 m thick and 19.8 m long, and weigh roughly 750 tonnes.

Canals in the United Kingdom
There are approximately 5,630 km of canal and river navigations in the United Kingdom.

You could travel all the way from Ripon in North Yorkshire to Godalming in Surrey on inland waterways, a distance of 670 km.

Loads of work
The workforce on the Suez Canal (opened 1869) consisted of 8,213 men and 368 camels.